The Arran Coastal Way

Jacquetta Megarry

Rucksack Readers

The Arran Coastal Way

First published 2008 by Rucksack Readers, Landrick Lodge, Dunblane, FK15 0HY, UK; reprinted with updates 2011

Phone   +44/0 1786 824 696
Email: info@rucsacs.com
Website   **www.rucsacs.com**

The maps in this book were created for the purpose by Wendy Price Cartographic Services, based on 1946 Ordnance Survey mapping with additional information from the Royal Commission on the Ancient and Historical Monuments of Scotland, updated by Rucksack Readers from original field surveys in October 2007.

ISBN 978-1-898481-28-7

Designed in Scotland by **WorkHorse** (*www.workhorse.co*)
Printed in the UK by Ashford Colour Press on waterproof, biodegradable paper

Publisher's note

All information was checked prior to publication. However, changes are inevitable: take local advice and look out for waymarkers and other signage e.g. for diversions. Walkers are advised to check two websites for updates before setting out: *www.rucsacs.com/books/acw/* and *www.coastalway.co.uk*

Parts of the Way may be wet underfoot, others are remote, and the weather is unpredictable year-round. Boulder fields require great care, especially in the wet, and a few parts of the Way are not safely passable around high tide. You are responsible for your own safety, for ensuring that your clothing, food and equipment are suited to your needs and that your intended walk can be safely completed in daylight. The publisher cannot accept any liability for any ill-health, injury or loss arising directly or indirectly from reading this book.

Feedback is welcome and will be rewarded.

All feedback will be followed up, and readers whose comments lead to changes will be entitled to claim a free copy of our next edition upon publication. Please send emails to **info@rucsacs.com**.

The Arran Coastal Way: contents

Foreword

From the mainland, Arran is only a dozen miles across the Firth of Clyde, but on stepping ashore at Brodick pier, you feel as though you're entering an older, more peaceful world. The island has always held a special significance for me. It was while descending from the granite slabs of the A'Chir ridge some 35 years ago that I decided I wanted a job that would allow me to spend the rest of my life climbing mountains. The sun-kissed hills of Arran richly blessed me that day, as many times since.

Whilst Arran has always attracted climbers, some walkers are over-awed by the steep, narrow ridges and soaring pinnacles of the north island's mountains. Many would rather tackle something less dramatic, but still challenging enough to make an adventure. And so the 65-mile Isle of Arran Coastal Way was conceived.

Arran's geology makes it ideal for coastal walking. The shallow coastal fringe of its raised beach encircles the island, and the Coastal Way follows it closely, diverting inland only twice. Whilst much of the route follows footpaths and stretches of beach, parts involve road-walking, albeit a very quiet and pleasant road, mostly on the west of the island. The Way has evolved and improved over the years since I revisited Arran to open it in March 2003.

My own favourite section remains the toughest part of the route, from Kildonan to Whiting Bay, past Dippin Head. No footpath tames this section, although all difficulties can be bypassed on the road. With steep cliffs on one side and open sea on the other, there's something very satisfying in the uncompromising nature of the terrain. Rocky reefs run out towards the little lighthouse island of Pladda. This is rugged coastal walking at its finest.

Cameron McNeish

South towards Pladda from Kildonan

Planning and preparation

Best time of year

In theory, the Arran Coastal Way could be an all-year route because snow and ice are unlikely except on the high ground, even in winter. In practice, few would choose to walk it between November and March because of short hours of daylight, likely poor weather and limited accommodation.

In between, July/August tend to be busier months because of school holidays. The weather is apt to be drier in May/June, and September/October can be a good choice. The weather can be changeable: be prepared for all four seasons in one day!

The terrain

The Way encircles the island in a 65-mile (104 km) loop that lies mainly at or near sea-level, with only one real altitude gain. This is on Day 1, to the shoulder of Goat Fell at 630 m/2050 ft. This is the highest point of the Way, and on a fine day many will wish to continue uphill to enjoy the panorama from Arran's summit (874 m/2867 ft).

The going underfoot varies from tarmac road with grassy verge to tidal beaches with a mixture of boulders, shingle and sand. There are some constructed paths, forest roads and hillside tracks. Depending on the recent weather and state of the tide, in places you'll have to take care to avoid wet feet. On tarmac, you may prefer trainers to boots.

The percentage of road-walking is high in two sections, 3.4 and 3.5 (see Table 1), albeit along a scenic main road that carries surprisingly little traffic. Walk on the right-hand side so as to face oncoming traffic, and take to the verge or beach whenever suitable. Stay alert, especially near blind corners, and be prepared for the odd large vehicle.

Boulder field near Bennan Head

Days, stages and duration

We recommend walking the Way anti-clockwise. When road-walking, this puts you on the shore side of the main road, making it easy to take to the beach where preferable, and giving unobstructed sea views. We describe the Way starting from Brodick because that's where the ferry arrives, but you can start anywhere, or indeed complete it in sections as day walks, or spread it over a couple of long weekends.

We present the walk in seven sections on pages 33-59; Table 1 shows the daily distances. Consider allowing more than seven days for your holiday. For example, you may want at least a day to see the sights of Brodick (see pages 30-2) or to visit the Holy Isle: see page 22.

Table 1 *Distances for the Way's seven sections*		
	miles	km
Brodick*		
	8	13
Sannox*		
	9	14½
Lochranza		
	9	14½
Imachar		
	9	14½
Blackwaterfoot		
	7½	12
Lagg		
	10	16
Whiting Bay		
	12	19½
Brodick		
Total	64½	104

*Brodick to Sannox section shorter by 1½ mi/2½ km by low-level route: see page 34

Or you may want to take a day off walking, especially if the weather is poor. Conversely, in great weather, you may want the chance to explore the mountainous interior.

However, if you've only a week to spare, you can shorten the walk by a day or two. Combining the first two sections saves one day. It makes for a tough 17 miles (27 km), but is feasible for fit walkers who make an early start. Others can speed things up by using the low-level route instead of going over the shoulder of Goat Fell: see page 34.

You can save a further day by combining the third and fourth sections, perhaps using the bus or other transport to skip up to 10 miles (16 km) of road-walking between Catacol and the King's Cave car park. You could still include some splendid off-road walking by taking the Coire Lochan side-trip from Thundergay: see page 45. You could then use transport to Machrie, perhaps taking in the Standing Stones walk (page 17) and finish with the splendid King's Cave walk to Blackwaterfoot.

 Don't be misled by the modest distances in the table: difficult terrain makes for slow progress. Some of the off-road sections involve slow, tiring boulder-scrambling, and in certain places there is no safe passage at high tide: see page 9. If you don't like boulder fields you can avoid them, using escape routes to the main road.

If you're very fit, you could even walk the Way in four long, demanding days, over-nighting at Lochranza, Blackwaterfoot and Kildonan. Even in summer there would be little margin for error, and this is not recommended if you want to see Arran.

Before deciding your schedule, think through four constraints on timing: hours of daylight, tide times, tough terrain and (unless supported by a driver) the bus timetable.

Auchrannie Spa Resort, Brodick

Accommodation

Where you spend your overnights is another factor. Nowhere on Arran is much more than half an hour away from Brodick by car. In theory, if you plan carefully from the bus timetable, you could stay in Brodick or Whiting Bay for your entire holiday, using the bus to reach the start, and return from the finish, of each day's walk.

However, there's a choice of interesting hotels and B&Bs in many villages on the Way, and it would be a pity to miss staying in places such as Lochranza, Blackwaterfoot, Lagg and Kildonan. Budget options include the youth hostel in Lochranza and five campsites: see page 61 and below. For groups, there are bunkhouses at Brodick, High Corrie and Kilmory Lodge (Lagg).

A good compromise might be to spend a few nights each in two or three places, using the bus as needed, reducing the need to carry overnight equipment. Since there's no accommodation at Imachar, after section 3.4 you would need to stay elsewhere, for example Lochranza, Pirnmill or Blackwaterfoot.

Many independent walkers prefer to have their overnight baggage transferred; for details of this convenient service, see page 61. Several tour operators offer an Arran Coastal Way package; if you book one of these, baggage and transfer arrangements will already be in place: see page 61.

Finally, if you intend to camp, be aware that there are campsites at only five places on the Way: Glen Rosa (basic facilities, 1 mile/1.6 km from Brodick), Lochranza, Shiskine (2 miles/3.6 km from Blackwaterfoot), Kildonan and Lamlash. All are marked on our drop-down map. In addition, under the *Scottish Outdoor Access Code*, wild camping is allowed for a couple of nights anywhere that access rights apply, but various responsibilities accompany that right. See the panel on page 10 for more about the *Code*.

Waymarking

When this book was first researched (October 2007) waymarking was patchy and inconsistent. Many improvements were made in 2008-10, but you'll still need to be vigilant. Carry a compass and large-scale map: see page 62. Most of the time, if you keep the sea on your right, you are unlikely to become seriously lost, but your walk may be needlessly tiring or frustrating if you are off-route. Knowing that there's a main road on the cliff-top to your left is of little use if you don't know where the escape route is and you've unwisely ignored the rising tide and/or falling light!

Be aware that the tidal nature of Arran's coast means that in places there is no single best path. At low tide you may have an easier walk on firm sand or shingle, whereas at high tide you may be forced higher, to scramble over large boulders or amongst overgrown vegetation. This is all part of the Way's distinctive character: excessive reliance on waymarking won't work on Arran.

Calm water in Lamlash Bay, sheltered by the Holy Isle

Tide awareness

Local newspapers, hotels, bars and the VisitScotland Information Centre normally can tell you about tide times. High tide around the island varies from Brodick, but not by much (up to 25 minutes). Brodick Bay tide tables often give times in GMT; if so, add one hour when British Summer Time is in force: see page 61 for an online source.

There are two high tides daily, about 12½ hours apart, with two low tides in between. Roughly speaking, the high tides tomorrow will happen nearly an hour later than those of today, and so on, day after day.

High tides are higher, and low tides lower, shortly after full and new moon, especially around the spring and autumn equinoxes. Weather, wind and waves also affect how dangerous places such as Bennan Head or Dippin Head could be around high tide. If in doubt, don't push your luck: use an escape route.

The Scottish Outdoor Access Code

The *Scottish Outdoor Access Code* interprets access rights established by law, and took effect in 2005: see the panel on page 10. The Arran Coastal Way passes through countryside which provides a livelihood for its residents. It is your responsibility to show consideration for them and their livestock.

Lambing takes places between March and June: never disturb pregnant ewes, nor approach young lambs. Cattle can be fiercely protective of their young. Give them a wide berth, especially if calves are around.

Give livestock plenty of space, especially it they're with young

The Scottish Outdoor Access Code

Know the Code before you go ... Enjoy Scotland's outdoors - responsibly

Everyone has the right to be on most land and inland water providing they act responsibly. Your access rights and responsibilities are explained fully in the *Scottish Outdoor Access Code*.

Whether you're in the outdoors or managing the outdoors, the key things are to
- take responsibility for your own actions
- respect the interests of other people
- care for the environment.

Find out more by visiting **www.outdooraccess-scotland.com** or by phoning Scottish Natural Heritage; see page 61 for details.

Dogs

Responsible owners are entitled to take their dogs along the Way. However, think carefully before deciding to bring your pet. Dogs must be kept under close control, not only to avoid stress to livestock and wildlife, but also for their own safety. If you are walking with your dog on the lead, keep well away from cattle: both dog and owner are endangered by this combination. Before deciding to take your dog along the Way, consider these points:

1 Some sections of the Way have stiles that you will have to lift your dog over. This can be strenuous and/or awkward, depending on the dog's weight and attitude.

2 Many accommodations do not accept dogs: check carefully before booking.

3 If your dog fouls the footpath, please clear up after it.

4 Dogs may disturb ground-nesting birds or young mammals: keep your dog under extra-close control during the breeding season (April to June).

Your rights and responsibilities when walking with a dog are listed in the leaflet *Dog Owners* from Scottish Natural Heritage: see page 61.

Stile on the descent from Goat Fell

Travel planning

Most people arrive on Arran after a ferry crossing of 13 miles (21 km) to Brodick from Ardrossan: see Table 2 for distances. Even if you drive to the ferry, you don't need to take your car over if your main goal is to walk the Way. There's secure car parking at Ardrossan and a bus service on the island: see page 12. If you must take a car, however, advance booking is essential. There are at least 4 or 5 ferries daily (7 or 8 in high season), journey time one hour with a minimum check-in time of 30 minutes for vehicles, 10 minutes for pedestrians.

A smaller ferry plies between Lochranza and Kintyre, calling at Claonaig in summer and Tarbert in winter; vehicles must be booked in winter. Note that timetables change twice a year, usually in late October and March. For fares, timetables and bookings for all ferries, contact CalMac: see page 61.

Trains take about an hour to reach Ardrossan from Glasgow Central, where trains from the south and west arrive. (From the north and east of Scotland, trains arrive at Queen Street, a short transfer to Central.) Boat trains normally connect with the ferry. Stay on until Ardrossan Harbour, the end of the line.

If arriving by air, from Glasgow Airport transfer to Paisley Gilmour Street station in time to join the Glasgow boat train as above (journey time about 50 minutes). From Prestwick Airport, take a train to Kilwinning station, then change for Ardrossan. There are about 4 trains daily.

Table 2 Distances from various places to Ardrossan	miles	km
Ayr	20	32
Edinburgh	80	129
Glasgow (city centre)	35	56
Glasgow Airport, Paisley	27	43
Prestwick Airport	16	26

Bus and ferry routes

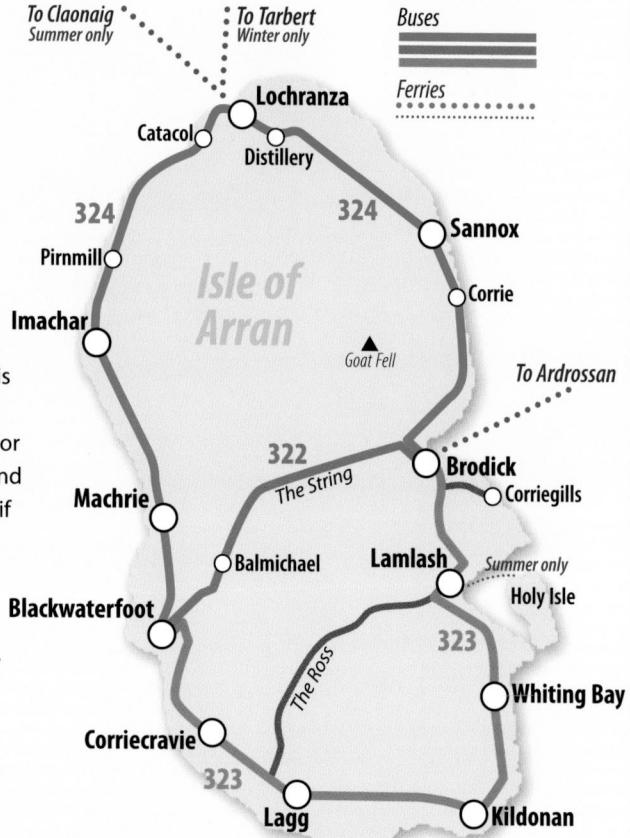

Arran is well served by its bus service and coastal road. Although there are only about 4 or 5 buses a day, the service is reliable, and timed to connect with ferries and other buses. For example, the String/South Island service waits for the ferry, and if you change at Blackwaterfoot you can connect with the String/North Island service.

To ride right around the island, use the Arran Rural Rover (unlimited bus travel for the day). The bus station is at Brodick Pier. Obtain the free *Area Transport Guide* leaflet for details: see page 61.

Fitness and preparation

If you haven't done much walking before, it's advisable to tackle the Way with someone who is experienced, especially in the use of map and compass. Well before you leave for Arran, do a few all-day walks to test your footwear and to build up fitness. If you'll be walking with a load, practise carrying a rucksack.

The Arran Coastal Way is difficult to compare with other long-distance routes. Taken slowly, and using the main road and cycle track to avoid the boulder fields and Goat Fell, it would be less demanding than the West Highland Way. Doing all the boulder fields and Goat Fell within 5 or 6 days would challenge many walkers' fitness and agility. Don't underestimate this walk. It's probably not the ideal choice for your first long-distance walk, especially if you plan to walk alone. For advice on choosing and buying gear, obtain our *Notes for novices*: see page 62.

Packing checklist

This list separates essential and desirable items. If you haven't worn your waterproof trousers recently, test them before you go, while there's still time to re-proof, mend or replace them. Gaiters are great for keeping boots and feet dry and mud-free, and for protection from brambles, nettles and bracken where ticks may lurk. Protection from the sun is also important: take both hat and sunscreen. Walking poles will be useful only if you already like them, and may be a liability at times, e.g. when crossing boulder fields. It helps to have rucksack loops that let you stow the poles while scrambling.

If you are camping, you will need much more gear (tent, sleeping bag and mat, food and cooking kit) and a much larger rucksack in which to carry everything. If wild camping, remember that safe drinking water needs to be boiled or purified. Using a baggage-handling service may be a better option unless you are experienced.

Essential

- rucksack with waterproof cover or liner(s)
- comfortable, waterproof walking boots
- specialist walking socks
- waterproof jacket and over-trousers
- clothing in layers (tops, trousers, jacket)
- hat (for warmth and/or sun protection)
- gloves
- guidebook, maps and compass
- whistle and torch (for emergencies)
- water carrier and plenty of water (or purification tablets)
- enough food to last between supply points
- first aid kit, including blister treatment
- toilet tissue (preferably biodegradable)
- personal toiletries
- insect repellent and sun protection
- cash and credit cards; there are 3 free cash machines in Brodick, but getting cash elsewhere can be difficult or expensive.

Desirable

- walking poles (if you normally use them)
- gaiters
- trainers, especially for road-walking
- spare dry socks to change into
- camera with plenty of spare memory or film
- spare camera batteries
- binoculars – useful for watching wildlife
- notebook and pen
- pouch or secure pockets for keeping small items handy and safe
- mobile phone.

> Mobile phone reception is very patchy in Arran. Never rely on one for personal safety. In 2011, the network with best coverage was Vodafone.

2·1 Scotland in miniature

Arran is Scotland's most southerly inhabited island, and its seventh largest, about 19 miles (30 km) long by up to 10 miles (16 km) wide. Its position in the Firth of Clyde makes it very accessible, a mere 13 miles from the mainland, just over two hours from the heart of Glasgow.

The moniker *Scotland in miniature* has some validity. Like Scotland, it is divided by the Highland Boundary Fault, with rugged mountains in the north, and fertile, low-lying land in the south. It has a cross-section of Scotland's habitats, and a wide range of its wildlife. Unlike Scotland as a whole, however, its population lives in coastal villages linked by the main road, and the island's interior is virtually uninhabited.

The number of Arranachs has fluctuated over time, with a peak of about 6500 in 1823, followed by progressive decline that has been checked in recent years. The present official figure is about 5000 residents, well over half of whom live in the three eastern villages of Brodick, Lamlash and Whiting Bay. Tourism is the main source of employment, and resident numbers are swollen by thousands of summer visitors.

The prevailing wind is south-westerly, and the climate moist and temperate. Mild winters allow palm trees and sub-tropical plants to flourish. Rainfall is high, especially in the east: Brodick gets about 89 in (225 cm) of rain per annum, compared to Arran's west coast's 70 in (170 cm) and Glasgow's 35 in (90 cm). However, May and June tend to be drier months, and nearly all the photographs in this book were taken during a single memorable visit in October 2007.

Most of the island has very noticeable raised beaches. After the last Ice Age, there was a massive release of weight when the ice melted. The land rose, creating raised beaches with former sea caves. In fact, there are two raised beach levels: the older 100-foot one, and the newer (10,000 year old) at about 25 feet above sea level.

Raised beaches provide the perfect platform for the A841 main road which encircles the island and is 56 miles (90 km) long. Together with two strategic roads across it, the String and the Ross, Arran is wonderfully easy to get around.

Arran's mountainous north, seen from Kintyre

Geology

Arran is the classic destination for field geology. Its rich variety of rock formations is unrivalled in the British Isles, perhaps in Europe. Students of geology come to Arran from all over the world to do their fieldwork.

As a mere walker, you can't fail to notice the remarkable variety of colours, shapes and formations in the rocks you see from the Way. There are colossal roadside boulders on the Corrie/Sannox shore, spectacular rock falls north of Sannox, and extremely old Cambrian schists in the north-west (south and west of Lochranza), up to 600 million years old.

There are dramatic caves and cliffs near Drumadoon Point, and impressive dark rocks around the Black Cave: see also page 52.

Sea caves north of Drumadoon Point

Scattered along the south coast are dykes of igneous rocks pointing like fingers out to sea, looking almost man-made. These relatively young rocks (about 60 million years old) have been left standing proud after weathering has ground down the older, softer Triassic rocks that surrounded them: see page 53 for another photograph.

Basalt dyke, with Ailsa Craig in stormy background

Hutton's Unconformity, near Lochranza

Arran played a pivotal role in the thinking of James Hutton (1726-97), the father of modern geology. Hutton visited Arran in 1787, searching for igneous rocks. He had already published his *Theory of the Earth* suggesting continuing tension between two processes, weathering down the mountains and upthrust by volcanic events, over long periods of time.

In 1645 Archbishop Ussher had calculated (from the Bible) that the earth began on 29 October 4004 BC, and Hutton grew up in an era when this Biblical timescale was accepted. On a walk near Newton Point, however, he noticed a strange angular rock formation: see page 41, third paragraph. The photograph above shows what became known as his *Unconformity*: the very old rocks (Cambrian schist) at centre left are sloping inland, whilst the younger sandstones to the right, further away, dip towards the sea.

Since sedimentary rocks are deposited in horizontal layers, it takes eons for geological processes (such as heat, pressure and folding) to force them up at an angle, and longer still for erosion to wear them down. Between the two kinds of rock at different angles, there is a huge time-gap, while erosion was slowly breaking down the rock into soil.

The gap is now thought to be far greater than Hutton realised: the Cambrian schist is 550-600 million years and the sandstone about 400 million years old. But Hutton's Unconformity proved his theory that the earth was far older than anyone had previously imagined. Much criticised in his lifetime, his radical ideas had a massive impact, not only in his lifetime, but also, 50 years later, on the thinking of the young Charles Darwin. Without Hutton's time span, Darwin's theory of natural selection would have been unthinkable.

2·2 Pre-history and history

The Stone Age farmers left many traces in hut circles, burial cairns and stone circles. Many standing stones – tall monoliths – are scattered around the island. The Way passes by ancient chambered cairns at Torrylin and the Giants' Graves: see pages 53 and 57.

Many forts or duns stand in prominent sites atop hills, dating from the Iron Age about 2000 - 2500 years ago. They were stone structures used for defence or residence, or perhaps both. Their shape is usually a distinctive oval mound, grass-covered, sometimes with stones visible. The Way passes several such forts, near Glen-ashdale Falls and the impressive Doon Fort at Drumadoon Point: see pages 57 and 48.

> **_i_** **Machrie Moor Stone Circles walk**
> _Leave the main road 250 m south of Machrie Water at the stile signposted 'Machrie Moor Stone Circle 1 mile': see page 47. Follow the track south-east across the fields, making a dogleg and passing the Moss Farm Road Stone Circle. Climbing slightly, you'll notice stones and cairns scattered over the moorland, once home to a settled agricultural community. It's actually 2 km from the A841 that you finally reach the stile to main site with its Historic Scotland interpretation board. Allow an hour for the round trip, more if you want time to wander about this atmospheric site._

Machrie Moor contains one of the finest range of ancient monuments in Scotland. Most prominent are six Bronze Age stone circles, about 3800-4000 years old and made of red sandstone or granite. Two of them stand on the sites of Neolithic timber circles which are 500 years older still. The moor also has scattered hut circles, chambered cairns and monoliths. The tallest of the monoliths is 18 feet/5.5 m high. The interpretation board helps to visualise what's missing where other stones have fallen.

By about 500 AD, Gaelic-speaking settlers from Northern Ireland, known as the Scotti, had extended their kingdom of Dalriada to south-west Scotland including Arran. They brought their Gaelic language, still spoken on Arran (by dwindling numbers) until the 20th century. In the 6th century, Irish missionary saints such as Brendan, Columba, Molaise and Donan brought Christianity.

Standing stones, Machrie Moor

From about 800 AD Arran fell under Viking rule, and its Viking legacy is obvious in many place names. In 1263, the Scots defeated the Vikings under King Haakon at the Battle of Largs, ending the era of Viking domination.

By 1371, Robert II (a Stewart successor to Robert the Bruce) had become King of Scots, and used Arran as his hunting ground while based at Brodick Castle: see page 32. Later centuries saw violent fighting between various feudal lords. The Way passes the impressive ruins of castles at Lochranza and Kildonan: see pages 42 and 54.

The Hamilton family's link with Arran dates from 1503 when James, Lord Hamilton married Mary Stewart, daughter of James II of Scotland. Their son James was created Earl of Arran, and Brodick Castle and most of Arran belonged to the family for centuries afterwards.

Major changes in agricultural practice led to the Arran Clearances of the early 19th century. Communal 'runrig' farms were abolished, more profitable sheep and deer introduced, and hapless tenants cleared ruthlessly, often by burning their homes. Some left for jobs in industrial towns, others for the New World, especially Canada. Migration was encouraged, with half the fare paid by the 10th Duke of Hamilton. There's a memorial to the 1829 voyage to Quebec City by 86 emigrants: see below.

In the late 19th century, Arran started to be seen as a holiday destination. Later, in the heyday of the Clyde steamers, visitors would rent a house for a summer month, and Arranachs would move into back quarters for the letting season. The steamers barely carried cars at first, but increasing demand led to frequent rollon-rolloff ferries and a trend for visitors to stay for shorter periods. The appeal of outdoor activities from golf to geology is still very strong, and many overseas visitors, especially from Canada, come to Arran to trace their families.

Arran Clearances Memorial, Lamlash

2·3 Scotch whisky and Arran

Whisky is made from just three natural ingredients: grain, yeast and water. A sequence of processes – malting, milling, mashing, fermenting and distilling – turns the grain into a strong colourless spirit, which is stored in oak barrels or casks before being bottled and sold as a precious amber fluid. Although a small amount of specialised whisky is bottled at cask strength (50-60% alcohol), most is mixed with water to reduce the alcohol level to about 40%.

By law, the label 'Scotch whisky' can be applied only if it has been wholly distilled and matured in Scotland, and has spent at least three years in the cask. There are two kinds of Scotch: malt and grain. Malt whisky is made only from malted barley, and is distilled in batches in a traditional copper pot still. By contrast, grain whisky may contain unmalted barley and other cereals, and is created in a patent still in a continuous, mechanised process. This section is about malt whisky.

'Single malt' means whisky that is 100% pure and from a single distillery, as opposed to blended whisky. Well-known brands are blends of grain and malt whiskies, with small amounts of many malts contributing up to 50%. The proportions of ingredients in each blend 'recipe' are a closely guarded secret.

Malt whisky is to grain as chateau-bottled wine is to table wine: it has more bouquet, has been matured for longer and is more expensive, sometimes much more so. Experts can identify a whisky uniquely just by 'nosing' it. The diagram below shows the sequence from malting to maturing.

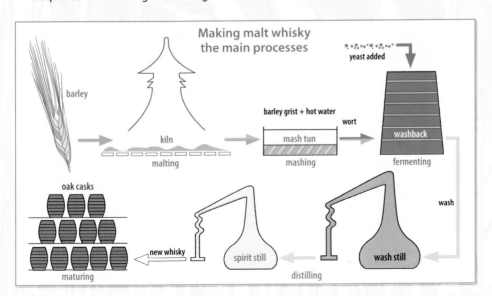

Making malt whisky
the main processes

yeast added

barley

kiln

malting

barley grist + hot water

wort

mash tun

mashing

washback

fermenting

oak casks

new whisky

spirit still

wash

wash still

maturing

distilling

'Malting' is the process of making the barley 'sprout' (germinate) by soaking, turning, heating and drying in kilns fuelled with peat. This breaks down starches and helps to convert them into sugars. Each distillery used to do its own malting: hence the distinctive pagoda shape of the malting house chimney. Nowadays most distilleries are supplied by centralised maltings, and Isle of Arran Distillers use Speyside barley, malted in Fife.

The dried malt is first ground or milled to make a coarse flour or grist. Then it goes for mashing in a large cylinder (the mash tun), where it's mixed with hot water and stirred to dissolve the sugars produced during malting. This produces a sugary liquid or wort, which is drawn off for fermenting, whilst the residue or draff is converted into dark pellets for cattle feed.

Fermentation takes place in large tanks called washbacks, where yeast is added and, under close temperature control, the sugar converted into crude alcohol. The process takes about 48 hours and the fermented liquid is called wash – a kind of sweet barley beer with about 5-7% alcohol by volume.

Distillation is the final stage before storage and bottling, and it takes place in pot stills. The wash is heated carefully so that most of the alcohol is vapourised whilst the water is left behind: alcohol has a lower boiling point (78°C) than water (100°C). The alcohol vapour rises up the wash still and passes along its swan neck to be condensed and collected in a water-cooled coil or worm.

Pot stills, Isle of Arran Distillery

The first distillation creates low wines, a portion of which is distilled again in a second, smaller spirit still to create high wines or new whisky. (The first and last portions of the batch are recycled into the wash still, and only the 'heart' of the run goes to the spirit still.) The whole process is controlled by a stillman using a spirit safe – a glass-fronted box through which the sprit passes after it comes off the still. (The box is kept locked by Customs and Excise: duty is not paid on whisky until it is bottled and sold.)

Water may be added to reduce the strength of the new whisky to 63.5%, the ideal strength for maturing it. Storage is in oak casks used previously for sherry or (more commonly) bourbon. Since oak is permeable, harsh elements of the new spirit escape and air and moisture get in.

Throughout storage, there is a loss of volume and of alcoholic strength known as the 'angel's share' – up to 2% per annum. For malt whiskies which are typically matured for 8 years or longer, this adds considerably to costs.

Stripped of its mystique and jargon, the process is essentially simple: malting, mashing, fermenting, distilling and maturing. However, every detail at each stage can affect aroma and flavour: the water source (ideally rising through peat and flowing over granite), the peat used in malting, the exact temperature and duration of the mashing, the precise shape and height of the pot still, as well as the time, temperature and proportions taken at each stage of distillation, the previous history of the casks and the microclimate during storage. Above all, the soft air and spring or burn water are considered vitally important to the final flavour. This may explain why nobody has succeeded in making anything that resembles Scottish whisky outside of Scotland, although many have tried.

Whisky-making on Arran

In the 16th century, the art of whisky-making had reached Scotland from Ireland, and gradually spread to suitable places throughout the Highlands and Islands. During the 17th and 18th century, Arran had a reputation for smuggling generally, and private stills were an accepted part of life.

In 1781, the Westminster Government outlawed private distilling and introduced punitive taxation, enforced by unpopular Excisemen. In the early 19th century, Arran had over 50 illicit stills, with a reputation for quality rivalled only by the famous Glenlivet. After a drastic reduction in duty in 1823, legal distilling became briefly worthwhile, but Arran's last distillery stopped production in 1837.

After a gap of nearly 160 years, the independent Isle of Arran Distillers Ltd built a new distillery in Lochranza, using traditional copper stills and wooden washbacks. The water source is naturally ideal: water from Loch na Davie drops 360 m/1200 feet to Lochranza, 'cleansed by granite and softened by peat'.

Distillery building was delayed slightly, to avoid disturbing a pair of golden eagles nesting in the glen above. They rewarded their hosts with a fly-past at the official opening in August 1995. The distillery started producing its award-winning 10-year old in 2006, and makes a range of other whiskies and a liqueur.

Distillery and Visitor Centre, Lochranza

On the A841 main road (with bus stop outside), the distillery is easy to find and only half a mile (800 m) from the Way. The Visitor Centre has an exhibition, with Eagle's Nest café upstairs. Tours begin with an audiovisual show and finish with a tasting; in 2010 the cost was £5.
Open daily March to end October 10.00 to 18.00, with tours leaving frequently; open Nov to Feb four days per week (Sat, Sun, Mon, Wed) 10.00 to 16.00.
Tel 01770 830 264, www.arranwhisky.com

2·4 The Holy Isle

Holy Isle is the shapely island that shelters Lamlash Bay. It's only about 2 miles long by half a mile wide (3 km by 1 km), but offers a great walk with rugged scenery and impressive views from its rocky summit, Mullach Mor (314 m/1030 ft).

The island is also home to an interesting collection of animal rare breeds, and has an important religious past, dating from the 6th century when Celtic Saint Molaise lived here as a hermit. There is historic evidence of a later Christian monastery and burial ground at its north-west end, though no traces remain.

In 1992, it was acquired by the Rokpa Trust, Tibetan Buddhists who run a variety of courses, retreats and environmental projects. Although the eastern half of the island is closed, visitors are welcome to complete a scenic circular walk: see page 23. Please keep to the well-signed footpath and respect the rules. The free leaflet explains the various requests: don't bring pets, alcohol or drugs, but do bring refreshments.

> **ⓘ** **By ferry to the Holy Isle**
> The ferry leaves from the Old Pier, Lamlash, 8 times a day in May to September, and the crossing takes about 10 minutes. Out of season, expect reduced service, maybe by arrangement only. All departures are subject to wind and tide. Booking is not normally necessary, but confirm your return plans with the skipper on your outward trip. In summer 2010 boats plied between about 10.00 and 16.45, and the adult return fare was £10. Email tomin10@btinternet.com or phone 01770 600 998 or 01770 700463.

In season, the ferry plies frequently from Lamlash: see panel. The boat lands at the converted farmhouse which opened as the Centre for World Peace and Health in 2004. Although it's feasible to walk the circuit inside three hours or so, a more relaxed visit takes longer. Either way, it would be a pity to leave Arran without visiting its miniature cousin.

You can normally buy refreshments and even can arrange to stay at the Centre: visit *www.holyisland.org* or phone 01770 601 100. The book *Holy Island* gives detail on its history, wildlife and the Buddhist project: see page 60.

Centre for World Peace and Health, Holy Isle

The walk

This circuit is described from the boat jetty clockwise, outward by the hilly spine, returning by the easy walk up the western coast. There are polite signs to guide you, and the path is well-defined, but walking boots are required. During or after wet weather, care is needed, especially on the steep descent at the southern end.

You may meet the rare breeds that run free and coexist peacefully. Hardy Eriskay ponies are descended from four animals introduced in 1981. The small brown horned animals are Soay sheep, a rare breed from the Outer Hebrides. They probably date from the Bronze Age, but were introduced to Holy Isle in 1970. The white, long-horned Saanen goats are more native, having lived here for seven centuries.

Summit of Mullach Mor (314 m/1030 ft)

Start your walk from the jetty, heading east uphill at the north side of the Centre. The path soon veers south-east, climbing the spine of the island to the cairn at Mullach Beag (246 m/800 ft). There are good views from here, but there's better in store.

The path descends south-east into the saddle, then climbs, steeply in places, to Mullach Mor. The trig point is decked with prayer flags and coins as offerings, and can be a great place to picnic in good weather. Its modest height belies its splendid unobstructed views over Arran, the Firth of Clyde with Ailsa Craig, and the Ayrshire coast.

Eriskay ponies running free on Holy Isle

The descent is steep in parts, but not protracted, and at its foot you have a choice. Turn left for a short diversion to Pillar Rock Lighthouse, or turn right to continue the circuit, soon passing the lighthouse cottages (used for the traditional Buddhist retreat of three years and three months).

Rock painting: Marpa the Translator

Turn right (north) in front of the retreat, to follow the coastal path which soon passes rocks painted with Buddhist images. Soon after the last of these, a small wooden bench which heralds St Molaise's Cave, just off to your right. Molaise (566-640 AD) was only 20 years old when he became a hermit here, later being ordained in Rome and then returning to Ireland. Centuries later, in 1263 the Vikings visited Holy Isle and Vigleikr cut runes with his name on the cave wall.

Just before the cave is the holy spring, known as the Healing Well, which looks more like a clear, rocky pool. There's a metal ladle for those who wish to sample its 'healing properties'. Between here and the cave is a huge level-topped block of stone, known as the Judgement Stone or St Molaise's Table, possibly used for preaching or announcing judgments. From the cave, it's only a mile (1.6 km) of flat walking back to the jetty and the Centre.

Summit cairn on Mullach Beag

2·5 Habitats and wildlife

Arran's mild climate and mixed scenery makes it home to a huge variety of plants and animals. Much of the island is recognised as a Site of Special Scientific Interest. With few predators and limited threat from human settlement, the animals are surprisingly approachable. In the space of a few days one October, I saw every creature photographed in this section, in most cases from nearby and in broad daylight.

Red-breasted mergansers

As ever, however, animals and birds are more active in the early morning and late evening, so these are the best times to seek them, if possible carrying binoculars and moving quietly. An interesting feature of the island is the complete absence of certain species that are commonplace on the mainland. You won't see any magpies, nor moles, foxes nor, mercifully, any grey squirrel: see page 28 for its charming red cousin.

The Way passes through three main habitats – coastal, woodland and upland – of which the first is clearly dominant.

Coastal

Much of the Way runs along or just above the beach. Arran has over 900 species of flowering plants, mainly concentrated on the raised beaches. At any time of year, wild flowers are blooming, with up to 50 kinds even in December. You'll see lots of ducks, including red-breasted merganser and eider duck: see above and page 27.

You are certain to see seal, both common and Atlantic grey, especially along the Corrie/Sannox shore, near Lochranza and also in the south, near Kildonan. Around low tide they cluster in larger groups; when the tide is in, lone seals bask on isolated rocks.

Common seal are smaller than grey, and not as long-lived (20-30 years, compared with 35 or more years for grey). Distinguishing them is easy if you're close enough to see their heads: the grey has a flat top to its head, whereas the common seal has a rounded forehead and V-shaped nostrils. From a distance, the common seal is smaller and sleeker, often arching its body; the grey looks more lumpish ashore.

Grey seal posing on rocks at high tide

25

Larger marine mammals include porpoise and dolphin. Porpoises are more common, usually swimming in groups some distance offshore. They are smaller than dolphin (up to about 6 ft/1.8 m) and you'll see their rounded backs and very small dorsal fin. Dolphins grow up to about 12 ft/3.5 m, have larger fins and are predators. They are more likely than porpoises to approach the shore.

In the same family (*cetaceans*) are whales, but they are much rarer. Minke whale, which grow up to 36 ft/11 m in length, occasionally visit Arran. Your best chance of seeing any of these marine mammals is in very calm weather, using binoculars.

Between August and October, you may be lucky enough to spot the large black fin of a basking shark: see above. These huge fish (up to 36ft/11 m) feed on nothing but plankton, and have no teeth. They are second in size only to whale shark, and internationally recognised as an endangered species: see page 61 for the website.

Arran has a good number of otters around its coast, but you need luck and patience to see this shy mammal. On land, they might be confused with mink, but are much larger, with a broad tapering tail. In the water, they leave a V-shaped wake when swimming. Your best chance is around dawn or dusk on a quiet section of coast. The otter in the photograph below is feeding on codling.

Basking shark

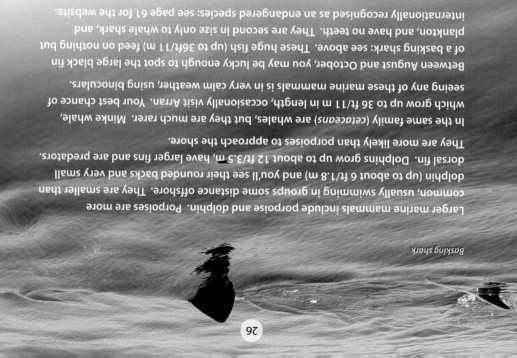

There's a wide range of sea birds, including gulls, fulmar and gannet. The gannet is easily recognised by its amazing aerobatics: they glide low over the water, hunting, then climb very high, folding their wings to dive-bomb their prey at speeds of over 80 kph (50 mph).

If you see large black birds standing on rocks with their wings outstretched or diving for fish, they are probably shag or cormorant. Shag are smaller and more common here; cormorant are distinguished by a heavier bill and white throat patch.

Eider duck (male)

The oystercatcher is a striking bird with a long orange bill and, in flight, an obvious M-shape in white-on-black. Unlike inland Scotland, where they are summer visitors, in Arran you'll see them year-round, sometimes in large flocks on the beaches. When disturbed, their piercing shrieks are unmistakeable.

A very different, crooning 'ah-ooo' sound is made by the eider duck, one of the world's largest and longest-living sea ducks. Drakes have the striking black and white breeding plumage shown in the photograph. Females are dull brown and mottled, well camouflaged for sitting on their nests, where they pluck down from their breasts for lining. In Iceland, this is still harvested for luxury duvets, jackets and eiderdowns.

Woodland

On the first day, the Way passes through a fine stretch of mixed woodland in Brodick Country Park *en route* for Goat Fell. There are mature spreading oak and beech, mixed with slender birch, ash and rowan. Conifers include Scots pine, the only pine tree native to Britain, with a sprinkling of imported species such as Sitka and Norway spruce. In spring, the colours in the Country Park's famous collection of rhododendrons are spectacular. In autumn, foliage and berries show their warm colours.

Brodick Country Park, with Castle

Red squirrel on birch branch

North of Sannox, and between Lochranza and Catacol, the Way passes through patches of mixed natural woodland. In spring, wild flowers flourish here, with patches of bluebells (wild hyacinth) and red campion. Wild primrose grows in clumps, with yellow flowers and crinkly bright green leaves.

Between Whiting Bay and Lamlash, the Way runs through planted conifer forest, with less variety of bird and plant life. Still, these trees are home to many birds, including coal tits and birds of prey. The Way also passes the foot of Glen Catacol, home to two endemic species of whitebeam, rowan-like trees found nowhere outside Arran.

Arran is one of the last strongholds of the agile red squirrel, elsewhere threatened by disease and competition from its non-native grey cousin. They're quite easy to spot, especially in autumn when hoarding food for the winter. If you see stripped pine cones on the ground, they've almost certainly been chewed by red squirrels. They occur anywhere on the island, especially in Brodick Country Park, the grounds of Auchrannie and even on garden bird feeders.

Upland

The Way climbs through Brodick Country Park via moorland to the shoulder of Goat Fell. Ground cover is rough grass, with blaeberry (*bilberry*) and heather, in places also with bog myrtle. These provide important habitat for brown hare and grouse. Tall heather is important also for the hen harrier, which preys on small mammals and birds. Arran has 5% of the UK's breeding population of this beautiful raptor.

Gorse (or *whin*) grows in dense, spiny patches with yellow almond-scented flowers almost year-round. Thorny brambles (*blackberry*) flourish, providing a heavy crop of fruit in autumn. Lower slopes have huge areas of bracken, the commonest and most invasive of ferns, but Arran has over 45 other species of fern.

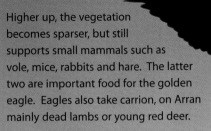

Golden eagle

Higher up, the vegetation becomes sparser, but still supports small mammals such as vole, mice, rabbits and hare. The latter two are important food for the golden eagle. Eagles also take carrion, on Arran mainly dead lambs or young red deer.

Eagle sightings are normally very rare and from afar, and visitors often mistake buzzard for eagle. The eagle has double the wing-span, and its flight looks very powerful, even from a distance, with an almost rectangular wing outline. A pair of these magnificent birds live above Lochranza, and the mountainous interior of the north island offers your best chance of a sighting.

If the eagle is the iconic bird of the Scottish Highlands, then the red deer is its iconic mammal. On Arran, they are commonplace, mostly kept in the northern half by a deer fence right across the island. In October, you will hear the loud bellow of the stags in rut, each one trying to collect a group of hinds and fighting off other stags with clashing antlers.

Red deer are easy to spot around Lochranza, especially out of season where they invade unprotected gardens, stroll on the golf course and even wade around the beach. On the mainland, they are normally seen only from a distance on the skyline. On Arran, they stay upland in summer, feeding on the sweet grasses, but in winter they descend for heather and other foliage. Culling is essential, to control numbers and to prevent the destruction of habitat which would lead to slow death by starvation.

Red deer stag with hind, from roadside, Lochranza

3·1 The starting point: Brodick

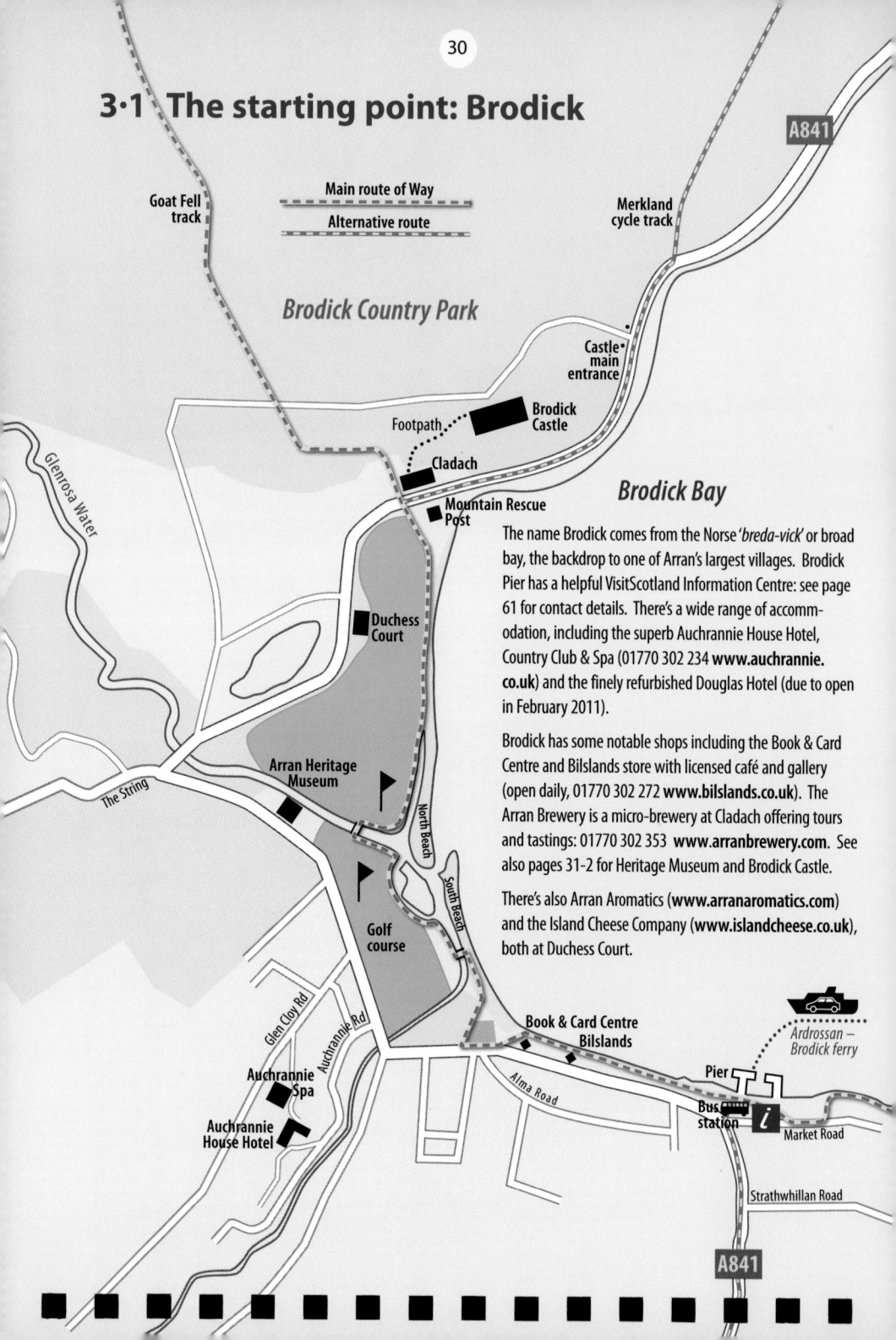

Goat Fell
track

Main route of Way

Alternative route

A841

Merkland
cycle track

Brodick Country Park

Castle
main
entrance

Footpath

Brodick
Castle

Cladach

Glenrosa Water

Mountain Rescue
Post

Brodick Bay

Duchess
Court

The name Brodick comes from the Norse *'breda-vick'* or broad bay, the backdrop to one of Arran's largest villages. Brodick Pier has a helpful VisitScotland Information Centre: see page 61 for contact details. There's a wide range of accommodation, including the superb Auchrannie House Hotel, Country Club & Spa (01770 302 234 **www.auchrannie. co.uk**) and the finely refurbished Douglas Hotel (due to open in February 2011).

Arran Heritage
Museum

The String

North Beach

South Beach

Brodick has some notable shops including the Book & Card Centre and Bilslands store with licensed café and gallery (open daily, 01770 302 272 **www.bilslands.co.uk**). The Arran Brewery is a micro-brewery at Cladach offering tours and tastings: 01770 302 353 **www.arranbrewery.com**. See also pages 31-2 for Heritage Museum and Brodick Castle.

There's also Arran Aromatics (**www.arranaromatics.com**) and the Island Cheese Company (**www.islandcheese.co.uk**), both at Duchess Court.

Golf
course

Glen Cloy Rd

Auchrannie Rd

Book & Card Centre
Bilslands

*Ardrossan –
Brodick ferry*

Pier

Auchrannie
Spa

Alma Road

Bus
station

Auchrannie
House Hotel

Market Road

Strathwhillan Road

A841

Isle of Arran Heritage Museum

This museum offers a comprehensive collection about Arran's history, people, culture and geology. Its lovely grounds descend to the Rosa Burn, and outdoor exhibits include farm machinery, a restored Brodick bathing hut and an antique petrol pump. The Cottage has parlour, bedroom, kitchen, wash house and milk house, all furnished to display details of domestic life in the early 20th century, using items donated by local residents and visitors.

Other buildings house recreated interiors – a post office with antique telephone exchange, a 1920s classroom and a smiddy with original forges, bellows and tools. Twice a year a blacksmith demonstrates the art of shoeing on a live horse. There are specialist sections on geology, archaeology and genealogy, with extensive displays and some audiovisuals.

Parlour in the Cottage, Heritage Museum

The museum is open daily 10.30-16.30, generally from March or April to October, but email or phone to check: info@arranmuseum.co.uk or tel 01770 302 636. The café is closed on Tuesdays, and in 2010 entry to museum and gardens cost £3 (seniors £2, gardens only £0.50). The website is at *www.arranmuseum.co.uk*.

Restored farm machinery, Heritage Museum

Brodick Castle

Arran's most popular tourist attraction is a rare example of a medieval defensive castle that later became a Victorian family country house. From 1503 the castle (and much of the island) belonged to the Dukes of Hamilton. In 1844 the 10th Duke commissioned architect James Gillespie Graham to extend and transform the castle into a gracious home for his eldest son, who had just married Princess Marie of Baden.

In 1906 the 12th Duke's only child, Lady Mary Louise Hamilton married the 6th Duke of Montrose, and the interior that you see today strongly reflects their interests and tastes. She and her son-in-law Major Boscawen were responsible for redesigning the gardens, which feature superb rhododendrons, four summer houses, gorges and waterfalls, a walled garden and an ice house.

Following the death of Mary, Duchess of Montrose, in 1957, the castle and gardens were passed (in lieu of death duties) to the National Trust for Scotland. Her surviving daughter, Lady Jean Fforde, continues to live in Brodick and wrote the Foreword to the excellent NTS guidebook on the castle. A wide range of good paintings, photographs, sporting trophies and *objets d'art* are displayed in the private apartments. The domestic details of the kitchen and servants' quarters are equally interesting.

Family mottos on the castle gates

The Castle is open daily, April-October, from 11.00, and the Country Park from 09.30 to sunset year-round. In 2010, castle admission cost £10.50 per adult: tel 01770 302 202. There are helpful staff in each room, but your visit is self-guided.

Brodick Castle, south facade, Victorian extension at left

3·2 Brodick to Sannox

Map	**Panel 1 (page 64)**
Distance	**8 miles (13 km)**
Terrain	**roadside pavement, footpath, forest track and mountain path, challenging in places by the Goat Fell route; the shorter, lower alternative combines main road and cycle track**
Grade	**flat path, then gentle ascent followed by stiff climb to 630 m/2050 ft at Goat Fell shoulder; steepish descent to sea-level; the cycle track climbs only to 130 m/425 ft**
Food and drink	**Brodick (choice), Cladach (bar and bistro), Corrie (shop and hotel), Sannox (hotel and bar)**
Side-trip	**optional climb of extra 244 m/800 ft to summit: see page 36**
Summary	**a potentially strenuous first day, with a big altitude gain and loss by the Goat Fell route, rewarded by amazing 360° views; in poor weather, choose the low-level alternative**

Brodick   Goat Fell   Sannox

5   2   1

8   3½   Corrie   1½

A841 / cycle track

The Way runs across Glenrosa Water

- Start from the ferry terminal, and walk along the beachside pavement west through Brodick for about 1 km, leaving the main road at the putting green (shown at lower centre of page 33) to pick up the Fisherman's Walk.

- The Walk sticks to the coastline, whilst the main road goes inland. The Way crosses three footbridges over streams, and the first one appears very soon on your left. After crossing it, head north across the golf course. Give way to golfers (and beware of golf balls) from here on.

- After 600m, cross the golf club's metal footbridge over Glenrosa Water. Turn right *immediately* to follow the path downstream.

- In 500 m, look for the discreet ACW waymarker pointing you left along a gorse-lined path leading to Brodick's north beach. Behind you there are lovely views over Brodick Bay, and ahead Goat Fell towers above you, whilst Brodick Castle nestles in the trees ahead.

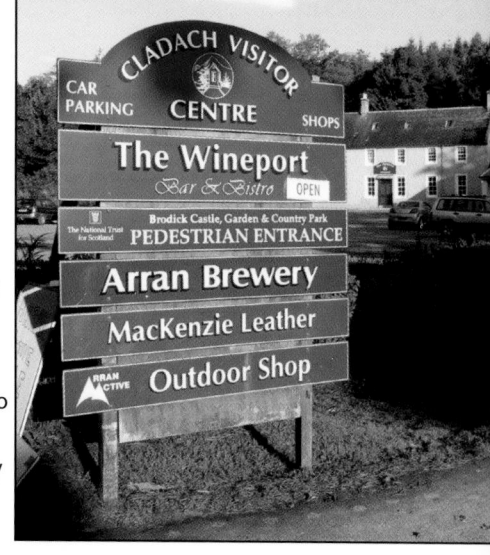

- At the end of the beach, cross the timber footbridge, and follow the path past the new Mountain Rescue Post. Cross the main road to the Cladach Visitor Centre with its cluster of shops – unless using the low-level alternative, see panel below.

- Walk through the car park, past the footpath to Brodick Castle, to the Goat Fell track, marked by a timber post. Follow this wide track gently uphill, which at first is lined with fine mature trees.

Low-level alternative (saves 2.5 km and 500 m of altitude gain)

In poor weather, or if you are unsure of navigation, an easier route follows the main road from Cladach past the main entrance to Brodick Castle. After 350 m take the Merkland Track and follow it for 500 m, where it forks. Bear slightly left to pass through the metal forestry gate.

At the "Maol Donn Loop" sign, bear right uphill and take the new cycle path to Corrie on your right. This climbs gently, passing through dense forest, and levels out. Once the path heads downhill, there are a few breaks in the trees, giving glimpses of the Clyde islands and the Corrie shore.

After a zig-zag descent, you meet the main road and turn left, within 300 m passing the junction where the Goat Fell route rejoins. You reach Corrie within 1 km (0.6 miles): see page 37, fourth paragraph.

- Various other trails are signed, to left and right: ignore them all, sticking to the well-signposted main track. Above Cnocan Wood, the path climbs north-easterly, narrowing and crossing some small streams that feed Cnocan Burn. It passes through heather and bracken, and is mostly well-drained, stony in places.

- About 3 km above Cladach, you cross a stream by footbridge and pass through a tall timber gate through the deer fence, entering land managed by the National Trust for Scotland. There are great views behind you to Holy Isle and the Ayrshire coast.

- The path continues to climb, in places steeply, heading northerly towards a ridge. You must identify this ridge, which runs west-east, to find your descent path to Corrie. The 2010 OS Explorer map still shows a cairn at the path junction (altitude 630 m, grid ref NR 998 415). Sadly it was removed many years ago, and the NTS (which owns Goat Fell) has not permitted a replacement marker. The two paths (from Brodick and to Corrie) merge at an angle of about 30 degrees: the photograph below should help.

- Depending on the conditions, your energy level and the time available before dark, this is your decision-point. If in doubt, head straight down to Corrie, almost easterly at first. However, there is no more rewarding viewpoint than Goat Fell's summit, and if you are tempted, read page 36 before deciding.

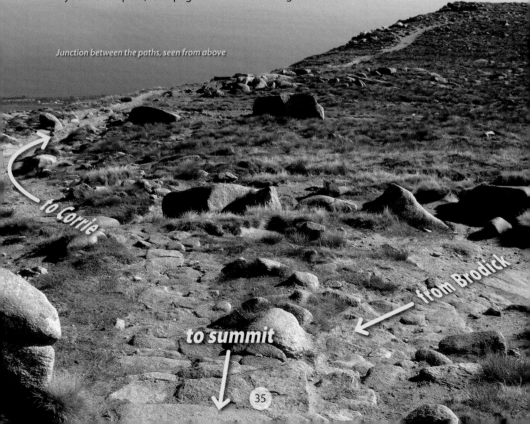

Junction between the paths, seen from above

to Corrie

from Brodick

to summit

Goat Fell: the summit

Looking northward from Goat Fell's summit

On a fine day, if time permits, don't miss Goat Fell's summit (874 m), the roof of Arran and only a further 244 m/800 ft of ascent above the path junction. The trail is narrow and rocky, a bit steeper and more strenuous than before, but in good conditions there is nothing to deter a hill-walker with any enthusiasm. You'll probably reach the summit in 30–45 minutes from the junction, but allow 2 hours for the round trip, so you've time on the spacious granite summit to enjoy the superb 360° views.

The summit location finder plate identifies not only the mountains of north Arran nearby, but also distant views of Jura, the Kintyre and Cowal peninsulas, the Clyde islands of Bute and the Cumbraes, the Ayrshire coast, Ailsa Craig and the coast of Northern Ireland. Many mountains of mainland Scotland can be seen when it's clear, from Ben Lomond (45 miles) all the way to Ben Lawers, some 74 miles off.

After enjoying the view, take care to descend by the way you came, leaving the summit area south then east, and looking out for the path junction. (There is also a northerly descent path via North Goat Fell, not described here but easily navigated if you have the skills.)

- Return to the path junction at NR 998 415 and bear left, descending towards Corrie down the rough boulder-strewn ridge that heads east-south-east at first. The path is rough, with a couple of awkward steps where you may prefer to use your hands.

- After about 700 m, the path swings to the left, northerly, and becomes more heathery as it descends to the Corrie Burn. Cross it by stepping stones, with care if it is in spate. On its far side, a clear broad path descends from your left, leading down from North Goat Fell.

- Turn right (east) down this path that follows the burn downstream, at first across open hillside. *En route*, you climb a ladder stile, go through a kissing-gate (passing through deer fences) and cross various streams. Lower down, the path is pleasantly surrounded by heather, bracken and bog myrtle.

- Eventually this path meets a broad, rough track where you bear left. It soon becomes metalled, after 500 m passing High Corrie, and descends steeply to meet the main road. Turn left, passing a bus stop to reach Corrie's village centre within 1 km.

- Walking north along the right of the main road, the journey through Corrie to Sannox is full of interest, both in geology and marine life. The rock formations are wonderful, both on the beach and roadside, and Corrie's wooden seal statue reminds you to look out for real ones, basking on the rocks. You'll also see sea birds and possibly even a basking shark if the sea is calm: see page 26.

- You will pass the Corrie and Sannox Village Hall, two small harbours, shops and Corrie Hotel with Ferry Rock opposite. Around the bend in the road, pass the Church and Primary School, and after 1 km you enter Sannox, past its quay and the Sannox Bay Hotel. Today's walk ends at the car park opposite the Glen Cottage, at the northern end of Sannox, where buses also stop.

Rocky shore near Sannox

3·3 Sannox to Lochranza

Map	Panel 1 (page 64)
Distance	9 miles (14.5 km)
Terrain	mixture of path and beach-walking, with some boulder-scrambling; hard going in places, especially during or after rain; final stretch is under 1 mile (1.6 km) of tarmac
Grade	coastal path with negligible altitude gain, but the boulders make it strenuous, especially around high tide when awkward moves are hard to avoid
Food and drink	Sannox (hotel and bar), Lochranza (sandwich bar and hotel)
Summary	a glorious day of off-road coastal walking, with many points of interest; there's an escape path about half-way, useful if you need to avoid the boulder field, but in normal conditions most walkers wouldn't find it too hard to complete the walk

Sannox — 2½ — Fallen Rocks — 4 — Laggan Cottage — 3½ — Rock Fall — 3¾ — Lochranza

escape path 2 — 2

North Sannox stepping stones

- Starting from the Glen Cottage bus stop, the route leads straight across Sannox Burn by the neat concrete cuboids of Sannox stepping stones. The route seems to lead directly to the beach, but just before it, turn left along a sandy path between gorse bushes, parallel to the shore.

- The path passes the garden gates of a few houses, and at first seems narrowly channelled between hedge and fence. You pass a tall white post, the southern end of the Sannox Measured Mile, which many famous ships have used for their timed trials. The path broadens out and runs parallel to a cliff face.

- About 1 mile (1.6 km) north of Sannox you need to cross North Sannox Burn. If the stepping stones look safe, use them but take care lest you slip. If the burn is in spate, the stones may be covered by fast-moving water: walk upstream to cross by the bridge and reach the picnic area on the far side.

- Pass through a gate, along a pleasantly wooded path with intermittent sea views, and large boulders to the left. After a picnic bench, you get your first glimpse of Fallen Rocks, an impressive landslip where colossal boulders tumbled from the cliffs to the sea. However there's no difficulty about picking your way through.

- Later the path opens out, with bracken-covered hills set back to the left and wide, open views over the Firth of Clyde to your right, with the islands of Bute and the Cumbraes prominent. Look out for basking shark and marine mammals: see page26. There are fine rock formations in this section, and also some caves up to your left.

- About 2.5 miles (4 km) after Fallen Rocks, you reach the wonderfully isolated white cottage at Laggan. On its far side, there's a waymarked escape route, a short-cut to Lochranza over the hill that avoids the Scriodan Rock Fall. Unless you are seriously struggling and it's high tide, this escape is unlikely to be necessary.

Fallen Rocks

Laggan Cottage

- The Way keeps right, along the shore, and 800 m after Laggan Cottage, you reach the ruins of Duchess Anne's Salt Pan, built in 1710. These workings are of a kind found in only one other site in Scotland, on the neighbouring island of Bute. Salt was vital to preserve meat and fish, and heavily taxed by the government. The discovery of nearby coal made it possible to extract the salt from sea-water. Arran salt was particularly pure, but the process was uneconomic and the Salt Pan became disused after only 20 years.

- The ruined building below is the pan-house, where the furnace and iron pans were. There are traces of smaller buildings nearby that stored fuel and salt, with workers' cottages inland and further north-west. Coal was dug from scattered pits, now water-filled. There's a plan of the workings in the Heritage Museum: see page 31.

Duchess Anne's Salt Pan

Cave in raised beach near Laggan

- One mile (1.6 km) after the Salt Pan, you reach the Cock of Arran, named after a huge sandstone boulder which, before its head fell off, resembled a crowing cockerel. There are caves up to the left, one known as the Picture or Smugglers' Cave (shown on the OS map as Ossian's Cave) with ship carvings and dates.

- Beyond the Cock lies the Scriodan Rock Fall, a boulder field that makes for slow, strenuous going. At mid or low tide, you can bypass problems by keeping low on the beach, but at high water you can't avoid a few awkward moves over large boulders.

- After passing Fairy Dell cottage, you start to see the headland beyond Lochranza. You're approaching Hutton's Unconformity, of great importance in the history of geology: see page 16. The path turns right at a small, bogus 'stone circle' towards the shore, then turns left to resume the coast towards Newton Point. Here, instead of keeping to the path across a tiny stream, walk back a few yards to the right and look for the unconformity photographed on page 16. It's at NR 935 521.

- After the unconformity, it's only 500 m to Newton Point: keep to the rocky shoreline to avoid the very boggy raised beach. The Point has a good location finder, dedicated to 'those who have done so much for geology and walking on Arran'.

- The path leads to a minor road that after 800 m turns right, skirting Loch Ranza to rejoin the main road. Turn right to continue the Way, or left to visit the distillery with restaurant: see pages 21 and 43.

Lochranza is Arran's most northerly village, linked in summer to Claonaig by the Kintyre ferry. Its ruined castle enhances its situation: see page 42. Surrounded by hills and facing north-east, it holds the British record for the shortest hours of sunshine in December. Visitors will probably remember it as the place where wild red deer wander around as if tame: see the photograph on page 29. Seals bask on the rocks of Loch Ranza's shores, and the coast is rich in flowers and sea birds. With a Field Studies Centre and Youth Hostel, the village often hosts groups of geology students from afar.

Red sandstone near the Cock of Arran

3·4 Lochranza to Imachar

Map	**Panel 2**
Distance	**9 miles (14.5 km)**
Terrain	**overgrown hill path at first, then mainly road-walking, taking to the verge or beach in places; the last 2 miles (3.2 km) are excellent beach-walking**
Grade	**Postman's Walk rises to 70 m (230 ft), then descends to the coast at Catacol, from where the Way remains almost at sea level**
Food and drink	**Lochranza (shop, hotel), Catacol (hotel), Pirnmill (tea room)**
Side-trip	**Coire Lochan: see panel on page 45**
Summary	**most walkers will relish the off-road start and finish of the day, but some may prefer to skip parts of the stretch (5 miles/8 km) of road in between, though traffic is light, and the views good**

Lochranza — 2 — 3 — Catacol — 4 — 6½ — Coire Lochan — Pirnmill — 3 — .5 — Imachar

Lochranza Castle from the east

ⓘ Lochranza Castle

The original castle was built for the MacSweens in the early 13th century, like Skipness Castle to help guard the Kilbrannan Sound. Most of the present ruins result from the C16th rebuilding. Allegedly, Robert the Bruce landed here in 1306 from Ireland, en route to his successful bid for the Scottish Crown.

The castle changed hands repeatedly, being extended, modified and fortified. In the 15-17th centuries, it belonged to the Earls of Montgomery. In the 1650s Cromwell put a garrison here, and in 1705 it passed to the Hamiltons. It has been disused since about 1800, and is cared for by Historic Scotland.

- From the T-junction, follow the main road north-west around the loch, past the Field Studies Centre and Youth Hostel. To visit the ruins of Lochranza Castle, turn right along its curved grassy spit: see panel on page 42.

- Continue along the road past the hotel, then just before the sign saying '115 yards to the Claonaig ferry', turn left up the farm road as waymarked.

- Within 200 m, the 'Postman's Walk' is signposted off to the right, just before the road swings up to Coillemore Farm, which includes parts of the oldest surviving house in Arran (built 1500-1700).

- The path heads steeply uphill at first, then levels out, giving wonderful views over the Kilbrannan Sound and Kintyre, and if it's clear, to the Paps of Jura beyond. The path is narrow and grassy, sometimes boggy, with fallen trees, bracken and rocks.

Waymarked tree, Postman's Walk

Isle of Arran Distillery, Lochranza

Catacol Row, seen from the Way

- After 800 m, the path swings south-westerly and the ground falls away steeply to your right, down an overgrown cliff face. You glimpse Catacol Bay with its neat row of white houses from a height of 70 m/230 ft. Don't lose height too soon: keep to the faint trod path and don't descend until well after you spot the tall ladder stile below, after you pass above the farther end of the row of houses.

- Catacol Row was built in 1843. Lord Rossmore had burnt his tenants out of their homes at Old Catacol because he wanted to make way for deer stalking. The tenants didn't want to abandon their farms for fishing, and rejected the houses. Each of the the 12 'Apostles' has a different pattern in its windows, so that fishermen's wives could signal with oil lamps to their husbands while out in boats.

- Once over the stile, turn right at the farm road, then pass through the gate at the main road. Turn left to continue along the main road, crossing it to face oncoming traffic. (You can take to the beach briefly here, but soon must cross a stream.)

- After Catacol Bay, the road crosses a river, the Abhainn Mor, undulating and twisting, with poor sight lines: walk with care. On the left, there are rugged rock formations, caves, and, after a couple of miles, a burial ground.

- There's a signpost to the Coire Lochan side-trip, see panel below. From here it's 1.5 miles (2.4 km) to the scattered village of Pirnmill. Its name derives from the pirns, or bobbins, manufactured here. The tall thin house where they were made stands inland, after the cafe and shop. After Pirnmill Primary School, walk 1 further mile (1.6 km) to Whitefarland before you finally leave the road, 5 miles (8 km) after Catacol.

West over Coire Fhion Lochan

- South of Pirnmill, pass a car park (on the left) and 150 m later reach the children's swings where a waymarker confirms the beginning of the path. This soon leads to the beach where you are free to choose from whichever surfaces – shingle, rock or sand – are on offer.

- After about 800 m, a pile of rocks marks an interesting walled graveyard on the left, which you can explore by climbing in from either side. Central in the photograph, the lichen-covered gravestone is to Captain John McMillan who died 1884 aged 48, erected by his widow.

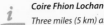

Coire Fhion Lochan

Three miles (5 km) after Catacol, a signposted path leads off left from Mid Thundergay to what is, in good weather, a lovely excursion to Coire Lochan. This small oval lochan is encircled by hills, with beautiful views to the west. The signpost leads to an access track where you follow signage through the kissing-gate. Follow the line of the fence until the footpath becomes clearer, north-easterly for about 800 m, over a ladder stile and across a burn. The route swings south-easterly and goes upstream alongside the burn to the shores of its source. It's a stiff climb to 330 m (1100 ft) and about 4 miles (6.4 km) round trip: allow at least two hours.

- An intermittent path may give easier going than the beach, but in places you may have to negotiate slippery rocks. There's a fine stretch of grassy path in a surprisingly wide flat section below the cliffs, and you'll see a couple of caves on the left.

- Throughout this beach walk, Kintyre's coast seems very close: from Imachar Point, to Carradale is barely 3 miles (5 km). A ferry used to ply from Imachar to Carradale and (to its south) Saddell Abbey.

- Near the end of the beach section, pass over two stiles, and rejoin the main road at a sharp bend that marks the end of this section.

- You are about 2.5 miles (4 km) south of Pirnmill and could walk back or, if you've planned your timing well, catch a bus to accommodation there or elsewhere. If flagging down a bus, stand somewhere that gives clear sight lines to the traffic, on the correct side of the road for your intended direction.

Burial ground on the beach south of Pirnmill

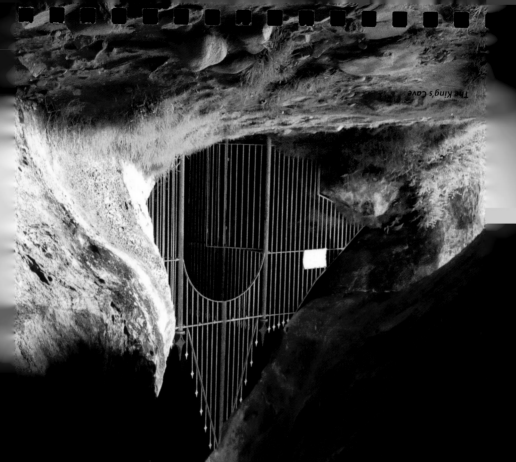

The King's Cave

Map	Panels 2 and 3
Distance	9 miles (14.5 km)
Terrain	mainly road-walking, followed by a delightful beach path that emerges at Blackwaterfoot
Grade	coastal road remains almost at sea level; once off-road, there's a slight climb (to 70 m/230 ft) and descent before the King's Cave, and a lesser climb near Drumadoon Point
Food and drink	Machrie (tea room), Blackwaterfoot (golf club, hotel, bakery)
Side-trip	Machrie Moor Stone Circles: see page 17
Summary	road-walking for 6 miles (10 km), then a glorious coastal path, past Drumadoon Point to Blackwaterfoot

Imachar — 5 — Blackwaterfoot — 3 — 1 — Machrie 1½ Car park — 5 — 8 — Imachar

- From the bend in the road near Imachar, continue south along the main road, using its right verge when gorse and brambles permit. In places, you may prefer to take to the beach as appropriate. The views are dominated by the cliffs of Drumadoon Point ahead, with Kintyre to your right.

- After Dougarie Lodge, an imposing white building with step gables, cross the Iorsa Water. Soon after, you start to see impressive caves on the raised beach to your left, formed by the sea some 10,000 years ago in Devonian sandstone.

- Further south you'll see more cliffs, also set back from the road. At a road junction 4 miles (6.4 km) after Imachar, bear left if you want to visit Auchagallon Stone Circle. But you are approaching the Machrie Moor Stone Circles side-trip. You could fortify yourself first with fresh local cooking from the Machrie Tea Room (which also serves the Machrie Golf Club), just between this road junction and Machrie Water.

- For the Machrie Moor side-trip, see page 17. Afterwards, it's almost 1 mile (1.6 km) to the car park with picnic area where the Way finally leaves the main road. The information board shows both the Way to the King's Cave and a newer return path for those making a circular walk. Bear right along the main path north-easterly, enjoying great views over Machrie Bay towards Beinn Bharrain: see front cover.

- After 800 m, the path descends steeply to the beach, and there are several former sea caves on your left; see photograph on page 15. The King's Cave is reached by unmistakable stone steps, and it has ornate ironwork railings. This palatial cave is supposed to have been used by Robert the Bruce *en route* to the Scottish crown in 1314.

The path descends to the beach

South to Drumadoon Point

- About 800 m after the cave, a huge rock stands on its own in a grassy clearing. It bears the footprints of a Triassic lizard-like dinosaur (*Chirotherium barthii*), some 200-240 million years old. There are great views across to Campbeltown with Davaar Island, and of Kintyre's southern tip, with Sanda, the 'spoon' island.

- Shortly after the footprints, there's a field clustered with strange piles of stones, a playful man-made addition to Arran's geology. As you approach, the sheer cliffs of Drumadoon Point look increasingly dramatic. They're about 60 million years old, known to geologists as a great example of a Tertiary sill.

- Keep straight on at the junction where a fainter path veers off to the right. Follow the Way inland, climbing the near side of the cliffs. At the top, there's a notice about keeping dogs on the lead. The path skirts around the back of the cliffs on which Doon (or Drumadoon) Fort is perched.

- To visit the 2000-year old fort, the largest on Arran, follow the Way through a metal kissing-gate, then bear right up a faint track to the large summit area. You'll see the exposed stones of its walls and enjoy a superb view from its commanding position.

- The path descends to a stile into Shiskine Golf Course. Turn left, keeping close to the fence.

- After 150 m, the golf club road crosses a burn. Turn right, downstream, to pick up the beachside road.

- Exit the golf club straight ahead along the minor road until it meets the main road. Here you turn right, soon reaching the Best Western Kinloch Hotel. This may be a welcome refreshment stop: in addition to bar meals, the hotel has a tempting bakery at its back.

Waymarker at the edge of Shiskine Golf Course

Kintyre coast across Kilbrannan Sound

3·6 Blackwaterfoot to Lagg

Map	**Panel 3**
Distance	**7½ miles (12 km)**
Terrain	**over 5 miles (8 km) of beach-walking with a mixture of overgrown path and some boulder-hopping; the last 2 miles (3.2 km) of road-walking may seem a welcome change**
Grade	**coastal walking, no altitude gain until a minor climb to the road at Sliddery, then level until slight descent into Lagg**
Food and drink	**Blackwaterfoot (golf club, hotel and bakery), Lagg Hotel,**
Summary	**although a short distance with negligible altitude gain, this section can be challenging, especially in wet conditions, but it's rewarded by splendid sea views**

Blackwaterfoot   Lagg

5½   2

9   Sliddery   3

- Pass between the Kinloch Hotel and the beach along a minor road. After passing a few houses it gives way to a broad, stony path. Keep heading south around the bay, using the beach as appropriate, crossing streams by stepping stones. Look behind for great views across Drumadoon Bay and its beaches, with mountains beyond.

- You are approaching a headland, Kilpatrick Point, at first by a grassy path, sometimes overgrown with bracken and brambles. Once you've rounded the point, look out for three caves close together in the cliffs to your left.

- The middle one is known as the Preaching Cave. It was used from 1815-21 instead of the parish church, by a congregation who didn't like the minister imposed on them. They preferred to worship in this cave, led by one of their elders.

North-west over Drumadoon Bay

- There's a tortuous path through the vegetation, with only the occasional waymarker to reassure you that you are still on course. With a mixture of rock-hopping and path-finding, you round one small headland after another.

- Once you start to see the volcanic plug of Ailsa Craig to the south-east, you're more than halfway through today's walk. There are plenty of dark igneous dykes: see page 15.

Grassy path near Kilpatrick Point

- The rock and bracken foreshore gives way to fenced fields, fringed by a gravelly shore. Stick to the water side, below the fences, all the way past Corriecravie. You can just see its houses up on the cliff to your left.

- Pick up a track that winds through the disused gravel quarry until it turns inland. Leave it there, instead passing between two timber posts standing beside a gate. Walk along the beach past the next field.

- Turn left up the track towards two cottages, the first buildings you've been near since Blackwaterfoot. Pass the cottages and climb the track between fenced fields, to meet the main road at Sliddery Stores. Turn right to reach Lagg within 2 miles (3.2 km).

- The road dips to cross Sliddery Water by a bridge, and within half an hour reaches the road sign announcing Kilmory, which is effectively combined with Lagg. The bus stops outside Lagg Hotel, which offers refreshments.

Towards misty Ailsa Craig, from the south-west corner of Arran

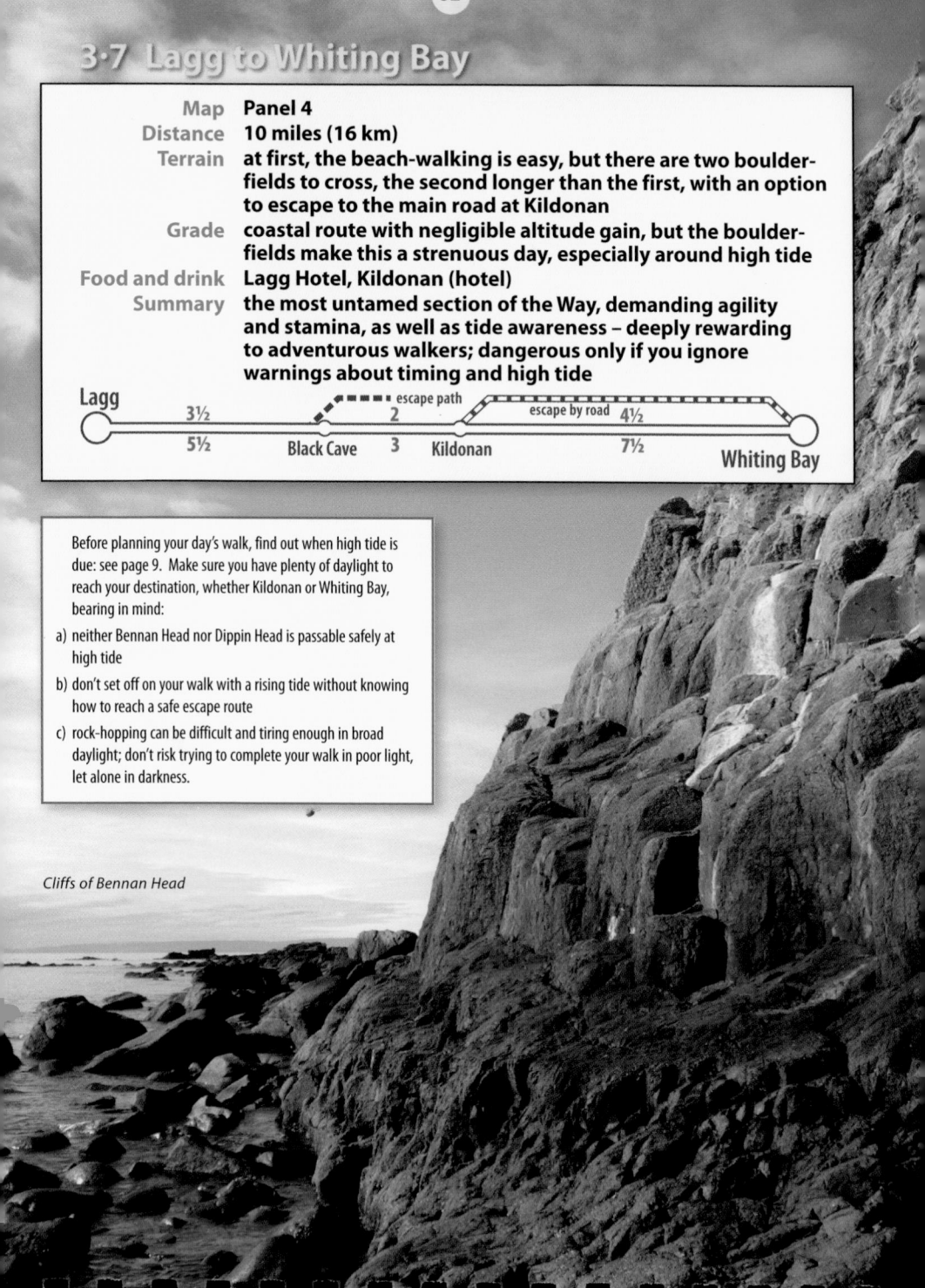

3·7 Lagg to Whiting Bay

Map	**Panel 4**
Distance	**10 miles (16 km)**
Terrain	**at first, the beach-walking is easy, but there are two boulder-fields to cross, the second longer than the first, with an option to escape to the main road at Kildonan**
Grade	**coastal route with negligible altitude gain, but the boulder-fields make this a strenuous day, especially around high tide**
Food and drink	**Lagg Hotel, Kildonan (hotel)**
Summary	**the most untamed section of the Way, demanding agility and stamina, as well as tide awareness – deeply rewarding to adventurous walkers; dangerous only if you ignore warnings about timing and high tide**

Lagg   3½   escape path 2   escape by road 4½
5½   Black Cave   3   Kildonan   7½   Whiting Bay

Before planning your day's walk, find out when high tide is due: see page 9. Make sure you have plenty of daylight to reach your destination, whether Kildonan or Whiting Bay, bearing in mind:

a) neither Bennan Head nor Dippin Head is passable safely at high tide

b) don't set off on your walk with a rising tide without knowing how to reach a safe escape route

c) rock-hopping can be difficult and tiring enough in broad daylight; don't risk trying to complete your walk in poor light, let alone in darkness.

Cliffs of Bennan Head

- From the Lagg Hotel, continue east along the main road, across the bridge over the river. Then turn right to follow the track downhill, signed to Torrylin Cairn.

- About 300 m from the start, the path divides: the branches rejoin later, but it's better to bear right. The path soon passes Torrylin Cairn, which you can reach through the gate on your left. These remains of a Neolithic chambered tomb were used for communal burial about 5300 years ago. There's a Historic Scotland interpretation board.

- Just after the Cairn, pass through the narrow wooden kissing-gate, down through the field and over a stile to the beach. Enjoy some of the easiest beach-walking so far, with firm sand and lovely views to the south, towards Ailsa Craig. About 800 m after the finger-post saying 'Bennan Head and Black Cave 1.3 km', look for the waymarked escape route that could take you uphill to the safety of the main road. Check your watch and tide time, and if all is well, proceed across the Bennan Head boulder field.

- About 500 m after the escape route, a huge boulder announces the Black Cave. It's Arran's largest cave, named after the dark basalt of these impressive cliffs. If you've timed your arrival for just after high tide, it's a great place to have a snack and check that sea level is really falling before tackling the main part of this boulder field. (If conditions are worsening, or the breakers too large, backtrack to the escape route.)

- Once past the Black Cave, the boulders continue but the views have changed: the village of Kildonan is visible ahead, and, less than a mile offshore, Pladda with its lighthouse. There's a succession of fine basalt dykes, with seals basking and posing.

Seals bask on a dyke, Pladda distant

Rainbow over Dippin Head

- The boulder field gives way to a mixture of sand, easy rock and an informal path, which emerges at the minor road. You've reached the western end of Kildonan.

- Follow the minor road along the sea front, past the Kildonan Hotel. Food and drink is available here, and it's a good place to review your progress and plans. Remember that the next boulder-field is longer and more tiring, with no escape route, and that Dippin Head is not passable at high tide. In good conditions, however, it's a rewardingly adventurous walk. Your alternative is to await a bus in Kildonan – or face over 3 miles (5 km) of road-walking.

- Just past the hotel, the Way descends a flight of steps to the beach. At first, the path is easy, then there's a mixture of grass, stony bits and some flat rock. Look for the picturesque ruins of Kildonan Castle above you on a cliff. Originally a tower house, probably used more for lookout than defence, it was mainly a Stewart stronghold. It changed hands many time, and was finally acquired by the Duke of Hamilton in the late 19th century.

Kildonan Castle, perched on its cliff

- The main boulder-field begins before the cliffs of Dippin Head and continues for up to an hour or so, depending on your fitness and agility. Yellow paint splashes on rocks may confirm that you are still on course.

- After you round the headland, you start to see your next objective, Largybeg Point. In places, the going may be easier on the grass above the boulders, despite the brambles.

- Progress gradually becomes easier, with smaller rocks and more of a path emerging. You still need to be vigilant: smooth rocks can be slippery when wet. There's a huge dyke and standing stones at Largybeg Point.

- Once past the point, it's only a mile (1.6 km) to the road. Holy Isle comes into view in the distance, and the going gets easier. Stay close to the sea, crossing several stiles on the way to the main road at Largymore.

- Turn right (north) into the southern end of Whiting Bay. The main Way turns inland from here, although there's a coastal alternative route: see map panel 4.

Cliffs of Dippin Head

North across Whiting Bay towards the Holy Isle

Glenashdale Falls

3.8 Whiting Bay to Brodick

Map	Panel 4
Distance	12 miles (19.5 km)
Terrain	good forest paths at first, then broad forest road for 4 miles (6.4 km), followed by minor road/pavement for 2.5 miles (4 km), then 5 miles (8 km) of beach and coastal path
Grade	short but steepish climb to 110 m (360 ft), then a long level stretch, gentle descent to the road at Dyemill, and the remainder at about sea-level
Food and drink	Whiting Bay (choice of cafés, pubs and shops), Lamlash (choice), Brodick (choice)
Summary	after an inland excursion with many points of interest, the Way descends to Lamlash and rounds Clauchlands Point in a final coastal walk westward into Brodick

```
  Brodick                              5                 8
  O─────────────────────────────────────────────────────O
  3   Whiting Bay        4           6½     Lamlash
                      Quarry
  5
```

- At the southern end of Whiting Bay, near the former Youth Hostel, the main Way turns left up the path with fingerpost for Glenashdale Falls and Giants' Graves: see panel.

i **The Giants' Graves**
After 500 m, turn left off the main path to climb up to these chambered cairns. The path soon turns into flights of steps, 360 in total, to reach the cairns at an altitude of 150 m (500 ft). At 5000 years old, these neolithic graves pre-date the great pyramids of Egypt. If you are interested in pre-history, the effort will be rewarded. Allow about an hour for the round trip.

- You walk on a well-drained undulating path through mixed woodland, with Glenashdale Burn on your right. The path crosses various side-streams and continues to ascend. After a steep climb and some flights of steps, it reaches an airy viewing platform with superb views over the Glenashdale Falls.

- After enjoying the falls, return from the platform and cross the burn by footbridge. Continue through the wood for 100 m or so, then turn right at a post through a gap in the stone wall.

- Descend on a path through the sitka forest: within 200 m you reach an Iron Age Fort on your right. You will see the exposed stones of its boundary wall, and the gap in the forest lets you appreciate its commanding situation.

- After the Fort, continue downhill, across a footbridge with side-falls on the left, then through a boggy area with alder and ash. After a few steps up, look for the marker post pointing sharp left, uphill. (There's a viewpoint bench below, to the right.)

- Within 100 m you emerge from the trees to meet a constructed path, where you turn left, uphill. (The waymarked circular walk turns right and descends to Whiting Bay.)

- The path soon meets the broad cycle track, where you turn right (north-east) for Lamlash. The forest road heads north, giving broad, easy walking. The views are open at first – to the right South Ayrshire, with Holy Isle ahead – then closed off by trees.

- After 1.5 miles (2.4 km) you reach Hawthorne Quarry. Climb the verge on the right to reach a picnic table with superb views across Whiting Bay to Holy Isle: see below.

- Just after the quarry, the track veers inland (north-west) and begins its gentle undulating descent. Clear felling has made gaps in the trees, especially on the right, and you pick up a stream to your left. The descent steepens, and the forest planting softens, with younger conifers and some birch, rowan and shrubs at its edge.

- Exit the forest by the concrete bridge, through the gate and past the Dyemill car park (which has picnic tables). The name derives from the former water mill which was used in the textile industry.

- At the Ross Road, turn right and descend towards the main road where you bear left. Arran FIne Foods factory and shop are at this junction. Continue along the main road to Lamlash, using the pavement at first on the left, then on the right.

- After the fire station, the coastal alternative route rejoins the Way via Cordon. The Way crosses Benlister Burn and picks up the greensward around Lamlash Bay. On the left, the Arran Clearances Memorial is in front of the row of houses: see page 18. The Old Pier has a tea room, and the Holy Isle ferry leaves from here: see page 22.

- Continue along the edge of the bay, keeping straight along the minor road where the main road turns left for Brodick. There's a long pavement stretch, with huge variety in the houses and gardens of the northern fringe of Lamlash.

- About 2 km after the main road turns left for Brodick, the minor road you are following turns left inland. Leave it here, instead keeping straight on through a wooden pedestrian gate along a farm track (muddy in places).

- A further 1 km after the gate, you reach Clauchlands Point with Hamilton Rock to its east: see below. Two World War II look-out shelters ('pill-boxes') are above, to your left: see page 59. Keep to the shore, and after rounding the point, cross a fence by a stile.

- Ignore the narrow path that leads left, steeply uphill to Dun Fionn Fort. Instead keep straight on along the coast, gaining a view of Goat Fell at the far side of Brodick Bay. The path narrows, passing through bracken, and after 2 km crossing a fence by a timber stile. You are near to the tiny settlement of Dunan.

Hamilton Rock, covered in sea birds

- From Dunan, you have a choice of route. You can turn left up the track to Corriegills, then turn right along the minor road until you reach the main road to Brodick Pier. Although on road, this undulating route is quite scenic.

- The alternative (not advised until a safe final path into Brodick is constructed) sticks to the coastline all the way. For this, keep to the access road until it approaches the very last house, where you turn right and descend to the shore. Follow it around Corriegills Point, keeping to the shoreline. Depending on the tide, use the faint path along the high water line or the sandstone foreshore.

World War II look-out shelter

- About 2 km after Corriegills Point, leave the landfill site on your left and, at the first opportunity, clamber up on to the minor road that leads to Brodick Pier.

Congratulations: you have completed the Arran Coastal Way.

Corriegills Point, with Brodick Bay in background

4 Reference

Origin of the Arran Coastal Way

The Arran Coastal Way was devised by Dick Sim of Brodick, and first documented by the late Hugh McKerrell of Lochranza in a 22-page booklet with supporting map. After the latter's death, his booklet went out of print, and the idea of a Rucksack Reader evolved. As author and publisher, I salute his expertise and the wealth of information that he presented, especially in geology and archaeology. It was a prime source for this book.

The Way was opened in March 2003 by Cameron McNeish, who later kindly wrote the Foreword to this book. Since the disbanding of the Arran Coastal Way Support Group, it has been looked after by the Arran Access Trust: email Kate Sampson of the AAT Ranger Service with any comments: **ksampson@nts.org.uk**.

Sponsors

The publisher wishes to thank the five Arran businesses that, in conjunction with VisitArran, generously supported this project:

Auchrannie Leisure (Brodick)
Bilslands (Brodick)
Book & Card Centre (Brodick)
Isle of Arran Distillers (Lochranza)
Best Western Kinloch Hotel (Blackwaterfoot).

Acknowledgements

The author thanks all those who assisted with her research trips and who commented on drafts, including Alastair Bilsland, Jim Cassels, Stewart Lambie, Kenny Morrison, Kerr Robertson, Dick Sim, Grace and Verner Small and Ramsay Weit; and is deeply grateful to Alastair and Alison Bilsland for their generous hospitality and practical support. Their efforts led to many improvements, but we are responsible for any flaws that remain. We welcome feedback, preferably by email to **info@rucsacs.com**.

Further reading

There's a wealth of books about Arran, but space to mention only a few. Once in Brodick, try to visit the Book & Card Centre for its outstanding selection of books of local interest. The TIC (see page 61) stocks books, maps and the hard-to-find leaflets mentioned below.

McLellan, Robert (1995) *The Isle of Arran* Pevensey Island Guides (David & Charles) ISBN 0-907115-91-8
Well-written and reliable, this 112-page book has been updated by Norman Newton and is a great source on heritage, landscape, flora and fauna, with many photos. It contains a section of place-names and their meanings, also further reading and index.

Wright, Allan and **Bonning, Tony** (2006) *Arran* ISBN 0-9551143-3-0
Originally a coffee-table hardback, this 96-page large-format paperback offers a superb collection of photographs with minimal but interesting text.

Kagyu Samye Ling Monastery (2007) *Holy Island* ISBN 0-978-906-181-24-9
Written by a volunteer, this 53-page book explains the island's history, gives background to the Buddhist project and paintings and describes the island's rare breeds. It has many photographs and will enhance your visit.

Two leaflets deserve special mention, available from the TIC, prices approximate:

Isle of Arran Trails: Geology   £0.25
Informative and readable introduction, with many photographs and map extracts.

Where can I see ...?   £1.65
Helpful 12-page booklet on where to see wildlife and plants, produced by the Arran Natural History Society.

Contact details

Phone numbers are shown as dialled from within the UK. Elsewhere, dial the access code, then 44, then the number minus its first zero.

Useful websites

The official Arran Coastal Way website is at
www.coastalway.co.uk
and lists accommodation and other services.
VisitScotland is Scotland's tourist board
www.visitscotland.com
There's a dedicated Arran website at
www.visitarran.com
Wildlife websites include COAST (Community of Arran Seabed Trust), promoting marine conservation in the waters surrounding Arran
www.arrancoast.co.uk
and one that organises an annual Wildlife Festival in the third week of May
www.arranwildlife.co.uk
Two websites are devoted to very special animals, red squirrel and basking shark,
www.highlandsquirrel.co.uk
www.baskingsharks.org
Scottish Natural Heritage is the government agency that publishes SOAC and *Dog Owners* (see page 10): phone 01738 458 545
www.snh.org.uk
Rucksack Readers hosts forums on many walks including the Arran Coastal Way: visit
www.rucsacs.com and click **forums**.

VisitScotland Information Centre

The only tourist information centre on Arran is at Brodick Pier, open 09.00-17.00 Mon-Sat (also Sundays in high season).
01770 303 774
brodick@visitscotland.com

Lochranza Youth Hostel

The 64-bed Lochranza hostel (01770 830 631) is open April to October, booking recommended, run by the SYHA. Membership is optional, and there's no upper age limit:
08701 553 255 **www.syha.org.uk**

Emergencies

In an emergency, dial 999 and be ready to state the problem, location and number of people affected. The police will connect you to ambulance, Mountain Rescue or Coastguard as appropriate.

Tide tables

Tide times for the current week are online at
www.bbc.co.uk/weather/coast/tides
then choose Scotland (area 4) and Port no 408 Brodick Bay. NB times are in GMT.

Service providers

As of 2010, we knew of one company that did baggage handling and two others with various self-guided packages for walkers. The list is bound to grow in future: please check our website for updates.

Baggage handling

Arran Coastal Way Baggage Co
01770 302 334   adamsonsuz@btinternet.com

Tour operators

Contours	**www.contours.co.uk**
Macs Adventure	**www.macsadventure.com**

Public transport

Caledonian MacBrayne
08000 66 5000   **www.calmac.co.uk**
for Arran, Kintyre and other ferries.

Buses to and within Arran are listed in a handy *Area Transport Guide* booklet (**www.spt.co.uk**) which also includes Ardrossan and Kintyre ferries and boat trains from Glasgow.

Traveline (for all public transport within Scotland, also to/from main places in the UK)
0871 200 22 33 **www.travelinescotland.com**

Scottish Citylink (Scottish buses)
08705 50 50 50 **www.citylink.co.uk**

Airlines

bmi	**www.flybmi.com**
British Airways	**www.ba.com**
easyJet	**www.easyJet.com**
flyglobespan	**www.flyglobespan.com**
Ryanair	**www.ryanair.com**

Online and printed maps

There's a detailed route map online at *www.rucsacs.com/routemap/acw/* that lets you zoom in to amazing detail in satellite view (with lesser detail in terrain view). Use it for planning or reminiscence.

Harvey's *Isle of Arran* waterproof map is at 1:40,000 (plus north island at 1:25,000). Ordnance Survey Explorer 361 covers the island at 1:25,000 though sadly as of 2010 it did not show the Way. Check for updates: *www.ordnancesurvey.co.uk.*

Notes for novices

Suggestions for novices on choosing and using gear are on our website: **www.rucsacs.com**. If you can't access this, send a suitably stamped addressed envelope to Rucksack Readers, Landrick Lodge, Dunblane, FK15 0HY, UK.

Photo credits

Auchrannie Leisure Ltd 7; **Niall Benvie**/rspb-images.com 29 (upper); **Fiona Barltrop** 15 (upper), 44 (lower), 46, 48; **Graham Chappell/Arran Graphics** 33, 42; **Matt Edwards** 25 (upper), 43 (lower); **Jacquetta Megarry** title page, 4, 5, 8 (all four), 9 (both), 10, 11, 15 (lower), 16, 18, 20, 22, 23 (both), 24 (both), 25 (lower), 27 (lower), 29 (lower), 31 (both), 32 (all), 34, 35, 36, 37, 38, 39, 40 (both), 41 (both), 43 (upper), 44 (upper), 45, 47, 49 (both), 50, 51 (both), 52, 53, 54 (both), 55 (both), 56, 57, 58, 59 (both), back cover; **Alex Pickup**/iStockphoto.com front cover; **Chris Sharratt**/chrissharratt.co.uk 26 (lower), 28; **Ben Slater**/iStockphoto.com 26 (upper); **Mark Townsend** 17; **VisitScotland** 14, 27 (upper).

Rucksack Readers

Rucksack Readers has published books covering long-distance walks in Scotland, England, Ireland and worldwide (the Alps, China, Peru and Tanzania). Its series *Rucksack Pocket Summits* is for climbers of the world's 'seven summits'. For more information, or to order online, visit *www.rucsacs.com*. To order by telephone, dial 01786 824 696 (outside UK dial +44 1786 824 696).

Visit our website for sample pages, gallery images, route maps, forums, online sales and discounts: *www.rucsacs.com*

Index

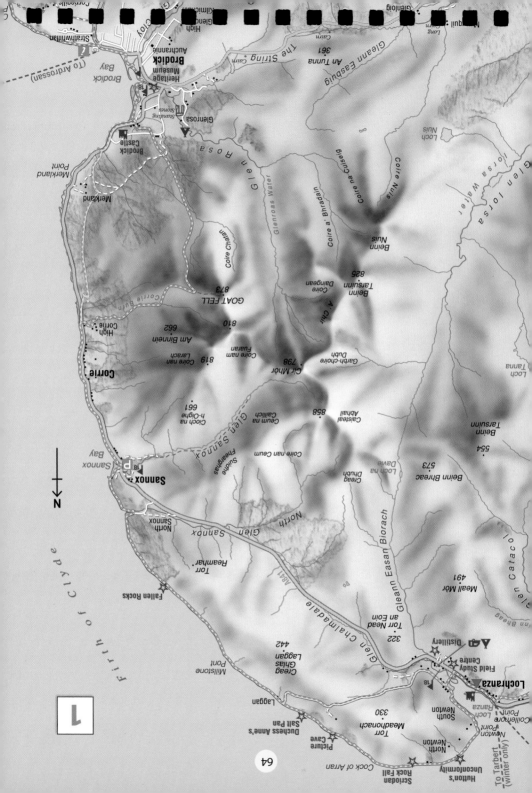